Where We Live

Germany

Donna Bailey

STECK-VAUGHN
LIBRARY
A Division of Steck-Vaughn Company

Hello! My name is Trudi.
I live in Bavaria in the south
of Germany.
Our home is near the border between
Germany and Austria.

We live on a farm near the mountains.
We raise cows and chickens
on the farm.
In the spring, we take the cows
to the meadows high in the mountains.

Every cow has a cowbell so that
we can tell where each cow is.
During the summer, the cows eat the
thick meadow grass and give us plenty
of rich milk.

When the grass in the fields has
grown very tall, we cut it and
pile it in stacks to dry.
The cows will eat the dried grass
during the winter.

In the autumn when it starts to get cold,
we round up the cows.
We bring them down from the mountains
and take them back to the farm.

The lead cow is always decorated with
flowers and ribbons.
She leads the way.
The other cows follow her.
The cows spend the winter in the barn.

Winters in Bavaria are very cold and
there is always lots of snow.
Sometimes it is easier to get around
on skis than in a car.

Everyone dresses in warm clothes and goes
sledding and skiing.
We have lots of fun on our sled.

Experts ski for miles over the mountains.
They get to the top of the ski runs
on a cable car.
This cable car goes to the top of the
Zugspitze mountain.

The Zugspitze is the highest mountain
in Germany.
From the top of the Zugspitze
you can see mountains and peaks
that are in Austria.

In the summer, we often visit our friends.
They rent a chalet in the mountains for
their summer vacation.
The chalet is made of wood and has flowers
in the window boxes.

We often go hiking in the mountains
during our vacation.
Dad knows the name of every peak.
Some of the mountains in Austria have
snow on them all year.

We also go swimming and canoeing.
The water in the mountain lakes
comes from icy streams.
The sun heats the surface of the lakes but
the deep water is very cold.

On November 10 we celebrate St. Martin's Day.
We make colored lanterns at school.
In the evening, we light our lanterns and
go singing from house to house.
The people at each house give us treats and apples.

The people of Bavaria like music.
Every town has its own brass band.
Music is an important part
of every German festival.

The biggest festival in Bavaria
is the Oktoberfest.
This festival is held every year in Munich.
The celebration lasts sixteen days.
Visitors from all over the world come
to enjoy the fun of Oktoberfest.

Oktoberfest starts at the end of September.
In the months before the festival, people are busy
putting up booths and tents.
During the festival, the fairground
is crowded with millions of visitors.

The festival begins on Saturday.
Horses pull decorated carriages and wagons
through the streets of Munich to the fairground.
Crowds of people watch
the colorful parade.

The horses that pull the wagons
are decorated with bells,
colored ribbons, flowers, and lace.

On Sunday, the second day of Oktoberfest,
there is a famous costume parade.
Men and women wearing the costumes of
their region get ready to
take part in the parade.

Hundreds of brass bands play in the parade.
The musicians wear traditional Bavarian
leather shorts and decorated suspenders.

People come from all parts of Bavaria to
take part in the costume parade.
Some of the men wear tall hats that are
decorated to show the kind of work they do.

Other people dress up in historical costumes.
They wear the kind of clothes that
people wore a long time ago.

At the booths around the fairgrounds,
hungry visitors buy
traditional German food.
This woman is selling bread, rolls,
and pretzels.

At this stand you can buy meatballs,
potato salad, Bavarian white sausages,
or fried chicken.
You can even try roasted ox meat.

Another popular snack is
grilled mackerel.
This man is cooking the fish
over a charcoal fire.

Some booths sell heart-shaped honey cakes,
candied almonds, and other sweets.
At other booths, tourists buy stuffed animals and
Bavarian hats as souvenirs to take home
to their friends.

Balloon sellers wander among the crowds.
Their huge mountains of balloons tower
high into the air.

While many people spend their time
singing and talking in the big tents,
others enjoy the carnival rides.

Children and adults enjoy
the bumper cars, the roller coaster,
and the Ferris wheel.

After dark, the fairground is lit up
with colored lights.
People stay to enjoy the fun
until late at night.

Index

Editorial Consultant: Donna Bailey
Executive Editor: Elizabeth Strauss
Project Editor: Becky Ward

Picture research by Jennifer Garratt
Designed by Richard Garratt Design

Photographs
Cover: Zefa
Fremden Verkehrsamt Tourist Office: 18, 20, 23, 28, 29, 30
Robert Harding Picture Library: 6, 21, 26
The Image Bank: title page (John P. Kelly), 2 (W. Bokelberg), 5 (Joseph B. Brignolo), 7 (H.R. Uthoff),
11 (H.R. Uthoff), 16 (Juergen Schmitt)
Spectrum Colour Library: 22, 32
Zefa: 3, 4, 8, 9, 10, 12, 13, 14, 15, 17, 19, 24, 25, 27, 31

Library of Congress Cataloging-in-Publication Data: Bailey, Donna. Germany/written by Donna Bailey.
p.   cm.—(Where we live) Includes index. SUMMARY: Describes life in the south of Germany, close to the
borders of Austria and Switzerland. ISBN 0-8114-2566-5 1. Bavaria (Germany)—Social life and customs—
Juvenile literature. [1. Germany—Social life and customs. 2. Bavaria (Germany)—Social life and customs.]
I. Title. II. Series: Bailey, Donna. Where we live. DD801.B347B25   1991   943′.3—dc20   91-22763   CIP   AC

ISBN 0-8114-2566-5
Copyright 1992 Steck-Vaughn Company
Original copyright Heinemann Children's Reference 1991

1 2 3 4 5 6 7 8 9 0 LB 97 96 95 94 93 92